Twenty to Make

Knitted Phone Sox

Susan Cordes

Search Press

First published in Great Britain 2013

Search Press Limited
Wellwood, North Farm Road,
Tunbridge Wells, Kent TN2 3DR

Text copyright © Susan Cordes 2013

Photographs by Vanessa Davies at
Search Press Studios

Photographs and design copyright
© Search Press Ltd 2013

Print ISBN: 978-1-84448-875-9
EPUB ISBN: 978-1-78126-163-7
Mobi ISBN: 978-1-78126-164-4
PDF ISBN: 978-1-78126-165-1

The Publishers and author can accept no
responsibility for any consequences arising from
the information, advice or instructions given in
this publication.

Suppliers
If you have difficulty in obtaining any of the
materials and equipment mentioned in this book,
then please visit the Search Press website for
details of suppliers: www.searchpress.com

Printed in China

Dedication
*My love and thanks to my mother,
Margaret, who taught me to knit, crochet
and sew, and has given me skills that have
provided a wealth of pleasure over
the years.*

Abbreviations

beg: beginning

C6F: Slip next 3 stitches on to a cable
needle, hold needle to the front of the work,
k3, then k3 from the cable needle.

DPN: double pointed needles

inc: increase (by working into the front and
back of the stitch)

k: knit

k2tog: knit two stitches together

knitwise: as though to knit

p: purl

p2tog: purl two stitches together

PM: place marker

psso: pass slipped stitch over

rem: remaining

rep: repeat

sl: slip, usually slip 1 stitch

st(s): stitch(es)

st st: stocking stitch (US stockinette stitch);
alternate rows of knit and purl. Unless
otherwise noted, always start with a knit row.

tbl: through back loop

WS: wrong side

*: repeat the instructions following the * as
many times as specified

Contents

Introduction

Mobile or cell phones come in all shapes and sizes, so what better way to personalise yours than with these easy to make phone sox. Not only will they help to save your phone from getting a scratched screen, they also provide a talking point (no pun intended!) when others see your crafted sock.

Every pattern is easy to follow and quick to make, whether you are a beginner or a more advanced knitter. Make sure that your phone is securely buttoned up so it will not fall out of your finished phone sock, and remember that different yarns produce different effects and that each knitter has a different tension. You may need to do a practice version to size the cosy for your particular phone.

Great to make as little gifts for friends or family, they use only a small amount of yarn with the sizes easily adjusted to suit most mobile phones.

You could even be adventurous and use the patterns as the basis for tablet computer cosies or spectacles cases – just have fun knitting and relax!

Knitting know-how

General notes

Most of the phone sox in this book are based on two basic shapes (shown right), which are designed to fit most phones. There are hundreds (if not thousands!) of different types and styles of phones, but knitting has the advantage of being slightly stretchy, which means that the sox are very adaptable. If your phone is particularly large or small, you may need to adapt the patterns a little.

I always use circular bamboo knitting needles. This type of needle is polished and the stitches slip off easily on to the other needle. They are easy to carry around to knit 'on the go!'

Yarn bobs are used to wind yarns on to instead of having lots of balls of yarn that twist and get in a mess. It makes the task of using different coloured yarns within one article much easier. When using smaller amounts of different colours, I always use yarn bobs.

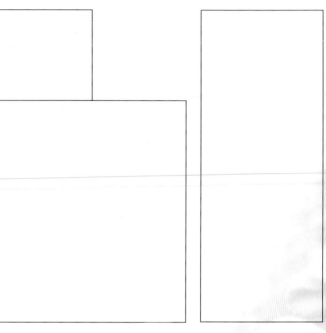

The two basic shapes for the projects. The size for each sock will vary, so these are only for guidance on shape. The diagram on the left is the basic shape for the sox on pages 8, 12, 18, 20, 22, 30 and 46. The diagram on the right is the basic shape for the sox on pages 10, 14, 16 and 26.

Tension

Every knitter will knit with a different tension; I suggest that you measure your particular phone and then cast on the number of stitches required. Knit a line or two to see how your tension compares to the pattern, then adjust accordingly.

Casting on with the finger or thumb method

1 Make a slip knot leaving a long tail. Put the slip knot on the knitting needle; hold the knitting needle in your right hand and use the tail to make a loop on your index finger (or thumb) of your left hand (this finger or thumb becomes the other knitting needle).

2 Insert the needle into the loop on your finger or thumb and knit the stitch.

3 Continue in this manner until you have the required number of stitches on your knitting needle.

Knitting techniques

Some of the techniques in the book may require a little extra information.

Moss stitch: Cast on an uneven number of stitches.

Row 1: k1, p1.

Row 2: k1, p1.

Rib: Ribbed knitting creates the look of vertical stripes. To achieve this, cast on an even number of stitches, then k1, p1 to the end of the row. For the next row, knit as the work presents to keep the pattern: where you see a knit stitch, knit; and where you see a purl stitch, purl.

Cable: Cabling takes a little practice and some patience. Suspend a number of stitches on a cable needle, either to the back or the front of your work, then knit the same number of stitches you have suspended, followed by knitting the stitches on the cable needle.

Examples of cabling instructions are C3F (cable 3 stitches by suspending 3 stitches to the front of the work) or C3B (cable 3 stitches by suspending 3 stitches to the back of the work).

Finishing and decorating your work

Sewing up: To sew up, use a knitter's needle with a large eye and a blunt tip – this stops the yarn splitting. When sewing up your knitted item using mattress stitch, always work in the same direction.

Running stitch: This is a simple embroidery stitch. Thread your sewing needle and begin by bringing your thread up from the underside of the material or knitted work, then taking the needle back down, leaving a space from the beginning of your work. Continue in this manner, making sure that the spaces between your stitches are even.

Mattress stitch: This method of closing the side seams is especially good when used with a piece of stocking stitch (stockinette stitch). Begin by piecing the two blocked pieces side by side (right side facing), stitch together the bars of the stocking stitch, keeping a straight line so that the seam is even.

1 Thread a big-eyed (knitter's) needle with a matching colour yarn and with your two pieces of work to seam lay them right side up. Insert the needle under the horizontal bar between the first and second knitted stitches of the first row of your knitting and gently pull together.

2 Insert the needle into the next row of the one knitted piecem, then the second and gently pull through. Continue in this manner until you have closed the seam. Weave your 'tails' in to complete.

Crocheting techniques

A few of the projects use some simple crocheting techniques detailed here.

Crochet hooks and crocheting: I use either metal or bamboo crochet hooks for a good result and ease of use. All crochet patterns begin with a foundation chain which is either a series of chain stitches or can be loops picked up from the edge of a knitted piece or chain stitches made into a loop. Always hold your hook and yarn comfortably and do not let the yarn become tight, especially when crocheting an edging.

Crochet edging: Most of the flaps on the phone sox have been reinforced with crochet edging to stop the edges curling. Pressing your sock with a warm iron over a damp muslin cloth will help.

The crochet edging used in these patterns is a simple attached chain stitch. Join your yarn into the first cast-off stitch and pick up a stitch to chain. Continue all the way around the opening with this attached chain stitch.

Attached chain stitch: Attach your yarn and loop on to your hook; working on the front of your piece put the hook through the two bars of the cast-off knitted piece and pull a loop of yarn through to the front side of your work. Slide the bottom loop off the hook.

Continue pushing the crochet hook through the knitted edge, pulling a loop of yarn to the front and sliding the bottom loop off the hook. To end, cut your yarn leaving a tail, then pull this tail through the last loop.

Detached chain stitch for loops and handles: Make a slip knot with the yarn. With your crochet hook still inside the slip knot, hook the yarn around the crochet hook and pull through the slip knot on the hook. This forms the first chain stitch. Maintaining a uniform tension, continue hooking the yarn around the hook and pulling through until you have the desired length of chain.

Purple Poodle

Materials:

1 x 50g ball double knit (8-ply) yarn – purple

1 x 50g ball double knit (8-ply) poodle yarn – variegated purple

Purple button

Embroidery thread

Tools:

1 pair 4.5mm (UK 7; US7) circular knitting needles

3.75mm (UK 8/9; US F) crochet hook

Knitter's needle for sewing up

Scissors

Tape measure

Instructions:

Sock

Using both balls of yarn and the 4.5mm (UK 7; US 7) circular needles, cast on 22 sts with the finger or thumb method.

Work garter stitch until the work measures 10cm (4in).

Cast off 11 sts loosely.

Work garter stitch on the remaining sts for 5cm (2in).

Cast off loosely.

I cord handle

Using both balls of yarn and the 4.5mm (UK 7; US 7) circular needles, cast on 3 sts with the finger or thumb method.

Row 1: knit.

Row 2: Do not turn the work – slide stitches to the other end of the needle and knit the row by bringing the yarn behind the work and starting with the first stitch. Give the work a little tug from the bottom after the first stitch to keep the shape.

Next rows: Rep rows 1 and 2 until cord measures approximately 18cm (7in).

Button loop

Use the crochet hook and purple yarn to make a loop of detached chain stitch (see page 7) sufficiently long to hold your button in place.

Making up

Weave in any loose threads, then close the seams on the side and bottom with mattress stitch and purple yarn. Next, make a detached chain stitch loop for the button (see page 7) and attach the button using the needle and embroidery thread. Sew the knitted I cord handle and button loop in place using the needle and embroidery thread.

Knitting note

Poodle yarn is usually composed of a combination of yarns (e.g. mohair and acrylic). Any item knitted in this type of yarn needs to be hand washed in cool water.

This unusual cosy uses poodle yarn, which produces a wonderful effect.

9

Moss-So-Simple

Materials:

1 x 50g ball double knit (8-ply) yarn – teal

Tools:

1 pair 3.5mm (UK 10/9; US 4) knitting needles

1 pair 3.25mm (UK 10; US 3) knitting needles

Knitter's needle for sewing up

Scissors

Tape measure

Instructions:

Using 3.25mm (UK 10; US 3) needles, cast on 20 sts in teal.

Rows 1–8: knit in rib (see page 7). At the end of row 8, k2tog [19].

Rows 9–14: Change to 3.5mm (UK 10/9; US 4) needles and work st st, starting with a knit row.

Row 15: k1, p1 to end of row.

Row 16: k1, p1 to end of row.

Next rows: Rep rows 15–16, until moss stitch (US seed stitch) pattern band measures 13cm (5in).

Next 6 rows: Work st st, starting with a knit row.

Next 8 rows: Change to 3.25mm (UK 10; US 3) needles and work rib.

Cast off.

Making up

Fold the work in half and close the side seams with mattress stitch.

A classy, classic design worked in moss stitch (US seed stitch) that will make a snug home for smaller phones. If you need to make it deeper to fit your phone, just knit more rib!

Elegant Pearls

Materials:

1 x 50g ball double knit (8-ply) yarn – cream

Toggle clasp, button or large hook and eye for closing

11 small pearl beads

Cream embroidery thread

Tools:

1 pair 4mm (UK 8; US 6) knitting needles

3.75mm (UK 8/9; US F) crochet hook

Knitter's needle for sewing up

Scissors

Tape measure

Instructions:

Using 4mm (UK 8; US 6) needles, cast on 28 sts in cream using the finger or thumb method.

Row 1: k4, p4 to end.

Row 2: p4, k4 to end.

Row 3: k4, p4 to end.

Row 4: p4, k4 to end.

Row 5: p4, k4 to end.

Row 6: k4, p4 to end.

Row 7: p4, k4 to end.

Row 8: k4, p4 to end.

Next rows: Rep rows 1–8 pattern until work measures 10cm (4in).

Cast off 14 stitches (keep pattern).

Continue working on the remaining stitches, keeping to the pattern for 3cm (1¼in).

Cast off loosely, then leave the last stitch on your needle to use as the first stitch for the crochet.

Making up

Transfer the final stitch on to your crochet hook and work the attached chain stitch method around the flap and opening, making a loop of 6 detached chain for the loop.

Close the side seams with mattress stitch, then attach the button using a needle and thread.

Weave in any loose ends.

Add pearl beads in the recessed squares (see detail), attaching them with needle and thread.

> **Knitting note**
>
> You may find it easier to stitch your pearls on to your phone sock before you close the side seams – just make sure you are attaching them to the right side.

*This design is so pretty and versatile –
it will go with virtually any outfit.*

13

Shooting Star

Materials:

1 x 50g ball double knit (8-ply) yarn – dark blue

Star button

Two gold star buttons

Gold coloured embroidery thread

Tools:

1 pair 4.5mm (UK 7; US 7) knitting needles

3.25mm (UK 10; US D) crochet hook

Knitter's needle for sewing up

Scissors

Tape measure

Embroidery needle

Instructions:

Using 4.5mm (UK 7; US 7) needles, cast on 15 stitches in dark blue using the finger or thumb method.

Work eight rows as follows:

Row 1: knit.

Row 2: purl.

Row 3: knit.

Row 4: k1, p4, k6, p4.

Row 5: knit.

Row 6: purl.

Row 7: knit.

Row 8: k1, (edge) k4, k1, p4, k5.

Next rows: continue rows 1–8 until work measures 23cm (9in).

Next row: With right side facing, k7, put the seventh stitch on to a 3.25mm (UK 10; US D) crochet hook and chain 6 sts (for the loop).

Put the last stitch back on to the right-hand knitting needle and knit to the end of the row.

Next row: purl.

Cast off loosely knitwise.

Making up

Close the side seams with mattress stitch.

Use the embroidery needle and gold-coloured thread to embroider two lines of running stitch across the sock, then attach a star button at the end of each line (see detail). Finally, add your button for the closure.

This pretty phone cosy is knitted in horizontal dash stitch. This type of knitting has occasional ridges of purl stitches on a field of stocking stitch (stockinette stitch), which helps to give this sock a lovely texture.

Black Cat

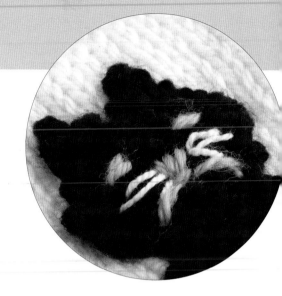

Materials:

1 x 50g ball double knit (8-ply) yarn – cream

Small amounts of double knit (8-ply) yarn – black, tan, green and white

Black embroidery thread

Tools:

1 pair 4mm (UK 8; US 6) knitting needles

1 pair 3.5mm (UK 9; US 4) knitting needles

Knitter's needle for sewing up

Embroidery needle

Scissors

Tape measure

Instructions:

Cat body

Using 4mm (UK 8; US 6) needles, cast on 6 stitches in black.

Row 1: knit.

Row 2: knit, inc 1 stitch at each end of row [8sts].

Row 3: knit.

Rows 4 and 5: Rep rows 2 and 3 [10sts].

Rows 6–13: Work 8 more rows garter stitch

Row 14: knit, dec 1 stitch at each end of row [6sts].

Row 15: knit.

Row 16: k2tog to end [3sts].

Row 17: knit, inc in every stitch [6sts].

Row 18: knit.

Row 19: knit, inc 1st at each end of row [8sts].

Rows 20–23: Work 4 rows garter stitch.

Rows 24–25: knit, dec 1 stitch at each end of rows [4sts].

Row 26: k2, turn, knit 1 row (ear).

Row 27: k2tog, fasten off.

Repeat rows 26–27 for other ear.

Fasten off.

Cat tail

Using 4mm (UK 8; US 6) needles, cast on 16 sts in black.

Cast off.

Sock

Using 4mm (UK 8; US 6) needles, cast on 20 stitches and work stocking stitch until work measures 24cm (9½in).

Cast off.

Change to 3.5mm (UK 9; US 4) needles and pick up 20 sts at cosy top, rib 6 rows, cast off.

Repeat for the other end.

Fold the work in half, stitch the cat and tail in place with the embroidery needle and thread, then close the side seams.

Making up

Weave in the loose ends, then use the small amounts of green, white and tan yarn to embroider the face as shown (see detail).

Close the side seams using mattress stitch.

This big black cat is for all lovers of cats and those who believe that black cats are lucky.

All Square

Materials:

1 x 50g ball double knit (8-ply) yarn – purple (A)

1 x 50g ball double knit (8-ply) yarn – lilac (B)

1 lilac button

Purple embroidery thread

Tools:

1 pair 4mm (UK 8; US 6) knitting needles

3.75mm (UK 8/9; US F) crochet hook

Knitter's needle for sewing up

Embroidery needle

Scissors

Tape measure

Yarn bobs

Knitting note

Twist the yarns or loops loosely across the back of the work to prevent holes appearing where new colours join.

Instructions:

Using 4mm (UK 8; US 6) needles, cast on 32 sts in purple yarn using the finger or thumb method.

Row 1: knit (wrong side).

Row 2: k4(A), k4(B) to end (right side).

Row 3: p4(B), p4(A) to end.

Row 4: k4(A), k4(B) to end.

Row 5: p4(B), p4(A) to end.

Row 6: k4(B), k4(A) to end.

Row 7: p4(A), p4(B) to end.

Row 8: k4(B), k4(A) to end.

Row 9: p4(A), p4(B) to end.

Next rows: Rep rows 2–9 until the work measures 10cm (4in). With right side facing, cast off 16 sts loosely.

Next rows: Keeping the pattern and colours the same, continue with the remaining sts to finish that block (7 colour blocks in total).

Next rows: Work st st in purple yarn for 3cm (1¼in).

Cast off loosely.

Making up

Weave in any loose ends and close the side seams using mattress stitch.

Using the crochet hook, attach chain stitch around the flap, making a loop of detached chain of 6 sts for the closing loop.

Work 30 chain stitches for the handle and join it to the side of the flap.

Attach the button using the needle and thread (see detail).

The chequerboard effect is much
simpler than it looks; and is a great
neutral design that will be set off by
the right choice in colours.

Love Hug

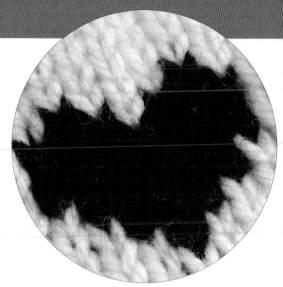

Materials:

1 x 50g ball double knit (8-ply) yarn – cream

Small amount of red double knit (8-ply) yarn wound on to a knitting bob

1 novelty house button

Cream embroidery thread

Tools:

1 pair 4mm (UK 8; US 6) knitting needles

3.75mm (UK 8/9; US F) crochet hook

Knitter's needle for sewing up

Scissors

Tape measure

Knitter's bobbin

Instructions:

Sock

Using 4mm (UK 8; US 6) knitting needles, cast on 33 sts in cream yarn using the finger or thumb method.

Rows 1–6: st st.

Row 7: k8 in cream, join in red for the heart and k1 in red, knit to end in cream.

Row 8: p23 in cream, then p3 in red, p to end in cream.

Row 9: k6 in cream, k5 in red, k to end in cream.

Row 10: p21 in cream, p7 in red, p to end in cream.

Row 11: k5 in cream, k7 in red, k to end in cream.

Row 12: p21 in cream, p3 in red, p1 in cream, p3 in red, p to end in cream.

Row 13: k6 in cream, k1 in red, k3 in cream, k1 in red, k to end in cream.

Row 14: p in cream.

Continue in st st in cream until work measures 10cm (4in).

Cast off 17 sts.

Continue working on remaining sts for 5cm (2in) to form the flap.

Cast off.

Handle and loop

Use the crochet hook and cream yarn to make a loop of detached chain stitch (see page 7) sufficiently long to hold your button in place. Make a second loop in the same way as a small handle for the sock.

Making up

Close the side and bottom seams with mattress stitch, then attach the button, and loop above the heart motif using the needle and thread. Use the needle and thread to attach the handle on the side as shown.

Knitting note

Make sure to twist the two coloured yarns so that holes do not appear in your heart!

This cosy is quite simple, and offers an introduction to intarsia knitting.

Funky Orange

Materials:

1 x 50g ball double knit (8-ply) yarn – burnt orange

1 novelty heart button

36cm (14in) of sequinned rick-rack braiding

Orange embroidery thread

Needles:

1 pair 4.5mm (UK 7; US 7) knitting needles

3.25mm (UK 10, US D) crochet hook

Knitter's needle

Scissors

Tape measure

Instructions:

Using 4.5mm (UK 7; US 7) needles, cast on 32 sts in burnt orange.

Pattern

Row 1: (RS) k1 (edge) *k1, p1, k1, p1*; rep from * to * to last 2 sts, k1, k1.

Row 2: work each st as it presents (see page 7).

Row 3: k1, *p1, k3*; rep from * to * to last 2 sts, p1, k1.

Row 4: work each st as it presents.

Row 5: (RS) k1 (edge) *k1, p1, k1, p1*; rep from * to * to last 2 sts, k1, k1.

Row 6: work each st as it presents.

Row 7: k1, *k2, p1, k1*, rep from * to * to last 2 sts, k1, k1.

Row 8: work each st as it presents.

Next rows: Rep rows 1–8 until work measures 13cm (5in).

Cast off 16 sts.

Change to garter stitch (all knit rows) for 5cm (2in).

On last row, cast off 8 sts then slip the one stitch on the RH needle on to the crochet hook and chain 6 detached chain stitches, slip the last stitch back on to the RH knitting needle and cast off remaining stitches.

Making up

Close the side seams with mattress stitch.

Use the needle and thread to attach the button, then the rick-rack braiding as a handle.

The surface of this phone sock (see detail) is seersucker stitch, which helps to give textural interest to the piece. This sock is aimed at those with an intermediate level of knitting expertise.

Sideways

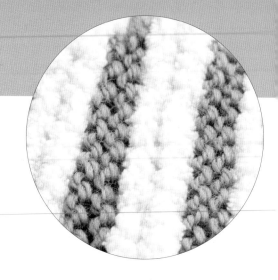

Materials:

1 x 50g ball double knit (8-ply) yarn – lilac (A)
1 x 50g ball chenille yarn – white (B)

Tools:

1 pair 4.5mm (UK 7; US 7) knitting needles
Knitter's needle for sewing up
Scissors
Tape measure

Instructions:

Increasing

Row 1: Using 4.5mm (UK 7; US 7) knitting needles, make a loop with lilac yarn (A).

Rows 2–3: Working in garter stitch, inc 1 st beg of every row until you have 5 sts.

Rows 4–5: Join in colour B and knit, increasing as before until you have 9 sts.

Rows 6–7: Using colour A, continue increasing until you have 13 sts.

Rows 8–9: Using colour B, continue increasing until you have 17 sts.

Next rows: Continue in this manner, increasing and alternating colours until you have 34 sts.

Decreasing

Next rows: Keeping to the same pattern of alternating colours as above, start decreasing 1 st at beg of every row until you have 2 sts rem.

Next row: k2tog.

Fasten off.

Making up

Close the side and bottom seams with mattress stitch.

> **Knitting note**
>
> When using two colours, twist yarns up the side of the work as you go. This keeps a neater edge.

This simple phone sock makes a soft cosy for your mobile phone and is knitted in garter stitch so it is great for the beginner.

Team Stripes

Materials:

1 x 50g ball double knit (8-ply) yarn – green (A)
1 x 50g ball double knit (8-ply) yarn – black (B)

Tools:

1 pair 4mm (UK 8; US 6) knitting needles
Knitter's needle for sewing up
Scissors
Tape measure

Instructions:

Using 4mm (UK 8; US 6) knitting needles, cast on 24 sts in colour A.

Rows 1–8: Work rib (see page 7) in colour A.

Rows 9–16: Join in colour B, joining in on the right side of work. Work rib.

Rows 17–24: Join in colour A, joining in on the right side of work. Work rib.

Continue in this pattern, alternating between colours A and B until you have nine stripes.

Cast off.

Making up

Close the side seams using mattress stitch.

Knitting note

Twist the colours up the side of your work as you go to make a neat edge.

26

This simple phone sock can be knitted in your favourite team's colours. It is worked in rib knit so that it keeps its shape well. The number of stripes will depend upon how deep you need the cosy to be for your phone.

Jolly Roger

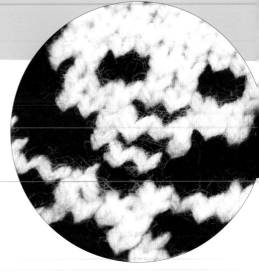

Materials:

1 x 50g ball double knit (8-ply) yarn – black (B)

Small amount of white double knit (8ply) yarn (W)

Tools:

1 pair 4mm (UK 8; US 6) knitting needles

Knitter's needle for sewing up

Scissors

Tape measure

Instructions:

Using 4mm (UK 8; US 6) knitting needles, cast on 18 sts in black.

Work st st until work measures 4cm (1½in).

Front

Row 1: k4(B), k1(W), k8(B), k1(W), k4(B).

Row 2: p2(B), p3(W), p7(B), p4(W), p2(B).

Row 3: k2(B), k4(W), k6(B), k4(W), k2(B).

Row 4: p4(B), p3(W), p4(B), p3(W), p4(B).

Row 5: k6(B), k2(W), k2(B), k2(W), k6(B).

Row 6: p7(B), p4(W), p7(B).

Row 7: k7(B), k4(W), k7(B).

Row 8: p2(B), p6(W), p2(B), p6(W), p2(B).

Row 9: k2(B), k3(W), k8(B), k3(W), k2(B).

Row 10: p2(B), p2(W), p4(B), p2(W), p4(B), p2(W), p2(B).

Row 11: k7(B), k1(W), k2(B), k1(W), k7(B).

Row 12: p7(B), p4(W), p7(B).

Row 13: k5(B), k3(W), k2(B), k3(W), k5(B).

Row 14: p5(B), p8(W), p5(B).

Row 15: k5(B), k1(W), k2(B), k2(W), k2(B), k1(W), k5(B).

Row 16: p4(B), p2(W), p2(B), p2(W), p2(B), p2(W), p4(B).

Row 17: k4(B), k10(W), k4(B).

Row 18: p4(B), p10(W), p4(B).

Row 19: k4(B), k10(W), k4(B).

Row 20: p5(B), p8(W), p5(B).

Row 21: k7(B), k4(W), k7(B).

Row 22: purl in black to end of row.

Row 23: knit.

Row 24: purl.

Cast off.

Back

Cast on 18 sts in black.

Work st st until work measures 13cm (5in) or the same length as the front.

Cast off.

Making up

Close the side seams using mattress stitch and weave in any loose ends.

The Jolly Roger phone sock should speak to everyone's inner rebel.

Curious Sheep

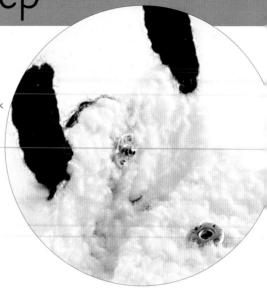

Materials:

1 x 50g ball double knit (8-ply) poodle yarn – cream

Small amount of double knit (8-ply) yarn – black

2 Seed beads for eyes

White embroidery thread for mouth

Small amount of toy stuffing

Press stud

Tools:

1 pair 4mm (UK 8; US 6) knitting needles

1 pair 3.5mm (UK 9; US 4) knitting needles

Knitter's needle for sewing up

Scissors

Tape measure

Embroidery needle

Instructions:

Sock

Using 4mm (UK 8; US 6) needles, cast on 16 sts in cream and work garter stitch for 9cm (3½in).

Next row: Cast on 8 sts at the beginning of the row, then continue in garter stitch until the work measures 15cm (6in) from the beginning of the work. Cast off. Close the side and lower seams.

Sheep head

Make one.

Using 3.5mm (UK 9; US 4) needles, cast on 9 sts in black.

Rows 1–10: st st, starting with a knit row, leaving a long tail.

Draw the tail through the stitches, and take the work off the needle. Stuff the head, then close the back of it. Use a needle and thread to attach seed beads for the eyes, then embroider a nose and mouth as shown using white thread.

Sheep ears

Make two.

Using 3.5mm (UK 9; US 4) needles, cast on 3 sts in black.

Rows 1–4: knit.

Draw up as for the head.

Knitting note

This pattern follows the left-hand diagram on page 6, but is worked sideways on.

Sheep legs

Make two.

Using 3.5mm (UK 9; US 4) needles, cast on 3 sts in black.

Rows 1–8: knit.

Cast off.

Making up

Use the embroidery needle and thread to attach the ears to the head, then attach the head to the body in the centre of the flap.

Roll each leg into a cylinder shape and attach them to the corners of the sock flap as shown, using the embroidery needle and thread.

Close the side seams using mattress stitch, then attach a press stud to finish (see detail) using the embroidery needle and thread.

This cheeky sheep looks great poking out of the top of a pocket or a bag.

Stripes

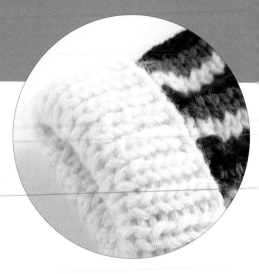

Materials:

Small amounts of double knit (8-ply) yarn – red
  (A), turquoise (B), cream (C) and green (D)

Tools:

1 pair 4mm (UK 8; US 6) knitting needles

1 pair 3.5mm (UK 9; US 4) knitting needles

Knitter's needle for sewing up

Scissors

Tape measure

Sewing needle

Instructions:

Using 4mm (UK 8; US 6) knitting needles,
cast on 20 sts in red (A).

Row 1: knit in colour A.

Row 2: purl in colour A.

Row 3: knit in colour B.

Row 4: purl in colour B.

Row 5: knit in colour C.

Row 6: purl in colour C.

Row 7: knit in colour D.

Row 8: purl in colour D.

Next rows: Continue with this colour pattern
until work measures 20cm (8in).

Cast off.

Pick up 40 sts on the side using colour C with
3.5mm (UK 9; US 4)needles.

Work rib for 5cm (2in) in colour C.

Cast off.

Making up

Close the side and bottom seams using
mattress stitch.

This jolly stripy sock is quick, simple and perfect as a gift.

Hot Air Balloon

Materials:

1 x 50g ball double knit (8-ply) yarn – blue (B)

Small amounts of double knit (8-ply) yarn – red (R) and tan (T)

Cream embroidery thread

2 novelty flower buttons

Blue embroidery thread

Tools:

1 pair 4.5mm (UK 7; US 7) knitting needles

3.75mm (UK 8/9; US F) crochet hook

Knitter's needle for sewing up

Scissors

Tape measure

Embroidery needle

Instructions:

Using 4.5mm (UK 7; US 7) knitting needles, cast on 44 sts in blue.

Rows 1–7: Work st st, starting with a knit row.

Pattern

Row 1: k6 (B), join in (T) for basket, k4(T) continue to end in (B).

Row 2: p in (B) until you reach the basket; change to (T), p4, p to end in (B).

Rows 3–4: st st in (B), starting with a knit row.

Row 5: k6(B), k4(R), k to end in (B).

Row 6: p33(B), p6(R), p to end in (B).

Row 7: k4(B), k8(R), k to end in (B).

Row 8: p31(B), p10(R), p to end in (B).

Row 9: k2(B), k12(R), k to end in (B).

Row 10: p30(B), p12(R), p to end in (B).

Row 11: k2(B), k12(R), k to end in (B).

Row 12: p31(B), p10(R), p to end in (B).

Row 13: k4(B), k8(R), k to end in (B).

Row 14: p32(B), p8(R), p to end in (B).

Row 15: k5(B), k6(R), k to end in (B).

Row 16: p3(B), p4(R), p to end in (B).

Row 17: k(B) to end.

Continue in (B) until work measures 12.75cm (5in).

Cast off.

Making up

Turn up 5cm (2in) of the sock at the opposite end to the balloon and slip stitch the seams closed. Secure the buttons in place as shown in the detail (above) using the sewing needle and thread. Use the 3.75mm (UK 8/9; US F) crochet hook to make two loops to fit around the buttons using detached chain stitch (see page 7). Weave in any loose ends then press lightly.

This phone sock has a folded wallet type design, with a flap for the phone to sit in. The hot air balloon would make it a fun present for a traveller.

Christmas Crystal

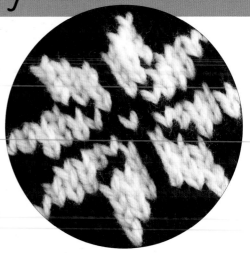

Materials:

1 x 50g ball double knit (8-ply) yarn – red (R)

Small amount of double knit (8-ply) yarn – white (W)

Tools:

1 pair 3.5mm (UK 10/9; US 4) knitting needles

1 pair 3.25mm (UK 10; US 3) knitting needles

Knitter's needle for sewing up

Scissors

Tape measure

Embroidery needle

Instructions:

Front

Using 3.5mm (UK 10/9; US 4) needles, cast on 19 sts in red.

Rows 1–6: st st, starting with a knit row.

Begin pattern:

Row 1: k6(R), k1(W), k5(R), k1(W), k6(R).

Row 2: p6(R), p2(W), p3(R), p2(W), p6(R).

Row 3: k6(R), k3(W), k1(R), k3(W), k6(R).

Row 4: p6(R), p3(W), p1(R), p3(W), p6(R).

Row 5: k2(R), k4(W), k1(R), k2(W), k1(R), k2(W), k1(R), k4(W), k2(R).

Row 6: p3(R), p4(W), p1(R), p1(W), p1(R), p1(W), p1(R), p4(W), p3(R).

Row 7: k4(R), k4(W), k3(R), k4(W), k4(R).

Row 8: p9(R), p1(W), p9(R).

Row 9: k4(R), k4(W), k3(R), k4(W), k4(R).

Row 10: p3(R), p4(W), p1(R), p1(W), p1(R), p1(W), p1(R), p4(W), p3(R).

Row 11: k2(R), k4(W), k1(R), k2(W), k1(R), k2(W), k1(R), k4(W), k2(R).

Row 12: p6(R), p3(W), p1(R), p3(W), p6(R).

Row 13: k6(R), k3(W), k1(R), k3(W), k6(R).

Row 14: p6(R), p2(W), p3(R), p2(W), p6(R).

Row 15: k6(R), k1(W), k5(R), k1(W), k6(R).

Rows 16–24: st st in red, starting and finishing with a purl row.

Row 25: Join in white, k1(R), k1(W) to end of row.

Row 26: p1(W), p1(R) to end of row.

Row 27: k1(R), k1(W) to end of row.

Row 28: change to 3.35mm (UK 10; US 3) needles and rib for 5cm (2in).

Cast off.

Back

Using 3.5mm (UK 10/9; US 4) needles, cast on 19 sts and work st st for 11cm (4¼in) in red.

Next row: Join in white, k1(R), k1(W) to end of row.

Next row: p1(W), p1(R) to end of row.

Next row: k1(R), k1(W) to end of row.

Change to 3.25mm (UK 10; US 3) needles and rib for 5cm (2in).

Cast off.

Making up

Close the side seams using mattress stitch.

A phone sock makes a great stocking filler, and having seasonal options means you will always have one to go with your outfit.

All Cabled Up

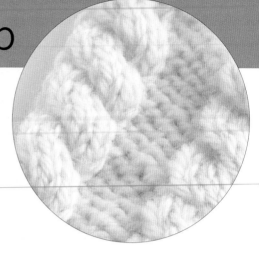

Materials:

1 x 50g ball double knit (8-ply) yarn – cream

Tools:

1 pair 4.5mm (UK 7; US 7) knitting needles

Cable needle

Knitter's needle for sewing up

Scissors

Tape measure

Instructions:

Using 4.5mm (UK 7; US 7) needles, cast on 18 sts in cream.

Row 1: p1, k6, p4, k6, p1.

Row 2: k1, p6, k4, p6, k1.

Row 3: p1, C6F, p4, C6F, p1.

Row 4: k1, p6, k4, p6, k1.

Next rows: Continue with this pattern until work measures 20cm (8in).

Next rows: Rib (k1, p1) until rib measures 2.5cm (1in).

Cast off.

Rejoin yarn to cast on end of cosy and pick up 18 sts.

Rib (k1, p1) until rib measures 2.5cm (1in).

Cast off.

Making up

Fold the sock in half and close the side seams with mattress stitch.

Knitting note

C6F: Slip the next 3 stitches on to a cable needle, hold the needle to the front of the work, k3, then k3 from the cable needle.

This simple phone sock makes a soft, thick cosy for your phone and is knitted using cable stitch.

Scottie

Materials:

1 x 50g ball double knit (8-ply) yarn – red (R)

Small amounts of double knit (8-ply) yarn –
black (B), white (W) and green

Tools:

1 pair 4mm (UK 8; US 6) knitting needles

1 set 3.25mm (UK 9; US 3) double pointed needles

Knitter's needle for sewing up

Scissors

Tape measure

Instructions:

Front

Using 4mm (UK 8; US 6) needles, cast on 20 sts
in red.

Rows 1–20: st st, starting with a knit row.

Begin pattern:

Row 1: k4(R), k4(B), k3(R), k4(B), k5(R).

Row 2: p6(R), p4(B), p3(R), p3(B), p4(R).

Row 3: k4(R), k9(B), k7(R).

Row 4: p7(R), p9(B), p4(R).

Row 5: k5(R), k7(B), k8(R).

Row 6: p5(R), p3(B), p1(R), p6(B), p5(R).

Row 7: k4(R), k1(B), k6(R), k5(B), k4(R).

Row 8: p4(R), p3(B), p1(W), p2(B), p4(R), p2(B),
p4(R).

Row 9: k11(R), k3(B), k6(R).

Row 10: p7(R), p1(B), p1(R), p1(B), p10(R).

Row 11: k10(R), k1(B), k1(R), k1(B), k7(R).

Row 12: p to end in red.

Rows 13–17: Work st st in red.

Cast off.

Back

Using 4mm (UK 8; US 6) needles, cast on 20 sts
in red.

Work st st for 14cm (5½in)

Cast off.

Making up

Close the side seams using mattress stitch.
Using 3.25mm (UK 9; US 3) double pointed
needles, pick up 40 sts around the top and rib
4 rows.

Cast off.

Make a small bow from green and red yarn and
stitch it in place on the dogs collar (see detail).

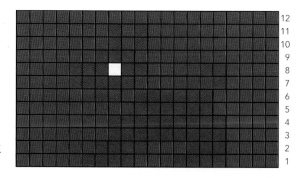

The template for the Scottie dog motif.

This cute Scottie dog phone sock has a space for the name of your beloved pet – or indeed, for the name of the phone's owner!

Halloween Pumpkin

Materials:

1 x 50g ball double knit (8-ply) yarn – black (B)

1 x 50g ball double knit (8-ply) yarn – orange (Or)

Small amount of green yarn (G)

Green and black embroidery thread

Needles:

1 pair 4mm (UK 10; US 3) knitting needles

1 set 3.25mm (UK 9; US 3) double pointed needles

Knitter's needle for sewing up

Scissors

Tape measure

Sewing needle

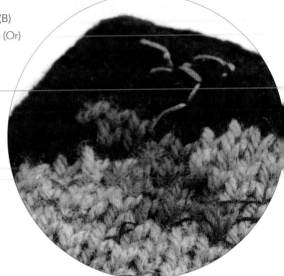

Instructions:

Using 4mm (UK 10; US 3) needles, cast on 40 sts in black.

Work st st for 2.5cm (1in).

Pattern

Row 1: k8(B), k3(Or), k3(B), k4(Or), k22(B).

Row 2: p21(B), p6(Or), p1(B), p6(Or), p6(B).

Row 3: k4(B), k16(Or), k20(B).

Row 4: p19(B), p18(Or), p3(B).

Row 5: k2(B), k19(Or), k19(B).

Row 6: p19(B), p19(Or), p2(B).

Row 7: k2(B), k19(Or), k19(B).

Row 8: p19(B), p19(Or), p2(B).

Row 9: k1(B), k19(Or), k20(B).

Row 10: p21(B), p18(Or), p1(B).

Row 11: k1(B), k17(Or), k22(B).

Row 12: p22(B), p16(Or), p2(B).

Row 13: k2(B), k9(Or), k2(G), k5(Or), k22(B).

Row 14: p23(B), p2(Or), p6(G), p7(Or), p2(B).

Row 15: k2(B), k8(Or), k4(G), k2(Or), k24(B).

Row 16: p26(B), p3(G), p8(Or), p3(B).

Row 17: k4(B), k8(Or), k4(G), k26(B).

Row 18: p23(B), p3(G), p5(Or), p9(B).

Row 19: k8(B), k3(Or), k29(B).

Work st st in black until work measures 14cm (5½in) from beginning of work.

Cast off.

Making up

Close the side seams using mattress stitch.

Embroider vine and lines on pumpkin using the sewing needle and green and black embroidery thread (see detail).

Using 3.25mm (UK 9; US 3) double pointed needles, pick up 60 sts evenly around opening and rib 4 rows. Cast off and weave in any loose ends.

The unusual side opening means that this design is fantastic for easy access to larger phones.

Golden Pineapple

Materials:

1 x 50g ball double knit (8-ply) yarn – orange

Small amount of green yarn

Needles:

1 set 3.25mm (UK 9; US 3) double pointed needles

3.75mm (UK 8/9; US F) crochet hook

Knitter's needle for sewing up

Scissors

Tape measure

Sewing needle

Instructions:

Using 3.25mm (UK 9; US 3) double pointed needles, cast on 35 sts in orange. Divide the sts evenly between the needles.

Begin moss stitch pattern.

Row 1: k1, p1 to end of row.

Row 2: k1, p1 to end of row.

Next rows: rep rows 1–2 until work measures 4in (10cm).

Next rows: Change to green yarn and rib 4 rows.

Next row: *k2tog, k3, k2tog (5 sts) on this needle, turn work around to complete this leaf.

Next row: p1, k1, p1, k1, p1 [5 sts].

Next row: k2tog, p1, k1, p1 [4sts].

Next row: p1, k1, p1, k1.

Next row: k2tog, k1, p1 [3sts].

Next row: p1, k1, p1.

Next row: k2tog, k1 [2 sts].

Next row: k2tog.

Fasten off.**

Next row: Move sts along needle so that you have 6 sts to work with for the next leaf. Join in green yarn and repeat from * to **

Continue in this manner until all sts have been worked off and the leaves complete.

Making up

Close the bottom seam using mattress stitch, then thread a length of yarn – use running stitches around the base of the leaves – and draw up. Weave in any loose ends.

Make a drawstring with the 3.75mm (UK 8/9; US F) crochet hook and orange yarn by working a row of detached chain stitch (see page 7) and changing halfway to green yarn.

Insert the drawstring around the base of the leaves (see detail).

This is a quirky design that is perfect for children.

Wise Owl

Materials:

1 x 50g ball double knit (8-ply) yarn – beige

Small amounts of dark brown double knit (8-ply) yarn

Small amount of flesh coloured felt for eyes

Small piece of brown felt for beak

Small amount of stuffing

2 black buttons

Press stud (snap fastener)

Needles:

1 pair 4mm (UK 8; US 6) knitting needles

Embroidery needle and brown sewing thread

Scissors

Tape measure

Instructions:

Using 4mm (UK 8; US 6) knitting needles, cast on 32 sts in beige using the finger or thumb method.

Row 1: Slip first stitch then purl to end.

Row 2: knit.

Next rows: Work in st st, starting with a purl row, until work measures 4cm (1½in).

Next row: With right side facing, k6, join in dark brown yarn, k4 (twist yarns loosely across back to prevent holes), knit to end in beige yarn.

Next rows: Continue with this colour pattern in st st until work measures 10cm (4in).

Cast off 16 sts.

Next rows: Work st st on the remaining sts until work measures 16cm (6¼in) from cast-on edge.

Cast off loosely.

Making up

Join the seams using mattress stitch. Attach a press stud (snap fastener) using a needle and thread, then cut out a triangle from the dark brown felt for the beak. Attach it using the needle and thread.

Make an eye by cutting out a pair of 2.5cm (1in) felt circles and filling them with toy stuffing. Place the eye on the owl's face and stitch it in place using buttonhole stitch and brown thread. Place a button in the centre of the eye and stitch it on. Add a second eye in the same way.

Cut several 8cm (3⅛in) lengths of yarn and tie them into the sides of the owl's head as ear tufts to finish.

Knitting note

Buttonhole stitch is similar to blanket stitch (although not the same) – it catches a loop of the thread on the surface of your work, then the needle is pushed back through the piece at a right angle. The stitch should look like an 'L'. Always keep even spaces between stitches.

This cheeky wise old owl
is a bit of a giggle!

Publishers' Note
If you would like more information on
knitting techniques, try:
Knitting for the Absolute Beginner by
Alison Dupernex, Search Press, 2012;
Twenty to Make: Knitted Beanies by
Susie Johns, Search Press, 2012